NO!

I0170053

No,
how and why you should say it!

Managing Editor:
Denny Portier-Terpstra

Contributors:
Norwyn Kam
Barbara J. Cormack
Bettina Pickering
Alyson Daley
Dr. Charuni Senanayake
Loren Schmal
Steve Rogers

Amarantine, Denny Portier-Terpstra, Norwyn Kam, Barbara J. Cormack, Bettina Pickering, Alyson Daley, Dr. Charuni Senanayake, Loren Schmal, and Steve Rogers asserts their moral rights to be identified as the authors of this work.

For more information: www.Amarantine.Life

ISBN: (Print)   978-1-939556-35-6
ISBN: (eBook)   978-1-939556-36-3

ISSN: 2515-7434 (Online)
ISSN: 2515-7426 (Print)

First published: March, 2018 UK

Contents

Denny's Deliberations

by
Denny Portier-Terpstra

I have been watching a new Dutch television show over the past few weeks, which is called "Going back to the year XXXX". In this show, local celebrities are spending time together with their family back in the days when they grew up. Everything in that show is set-up to represent some time decades ago; the house, the clothes, drinks and food, entertainment, technology, news, etc. And to make this experience real, all modern-day equipment like mobile phones, iPads and navigation are taken away from the family during this time.

The show is entertaining, because it brings back a lot of memories when you watch it. You may recognise a lamp from your parent's old house, the car that the neighbours used to drive, the first record you ever bought, or the favourite doll of your little niece. And as you listen to the celebrity parents sharing their memories, you're inclined to think back about your own Saturday evenings and Sunday mornings back in those days.

But the most interesting thing about this show, I think, is how people perceive living the lifestyle of the old days. One thing they all seem to agree on, is that life was SO SLOW! No matter how far you go back in time, people have never been living their life at today's speed, as they simply didn't have access to all the modern-day technology, tools and information available to us today. And whilst most modern inventions are designed to make our lives easier and free up our time, in actual fact they allow us to make our lives more complex, more hectic and more demanding!

Where families used to gather together around the TV to watch one show without breaks for an entire evening, these days we all watch our own shows on separate devices and we stay connected with the rest of the world via social media simultaneously, with frequent (commercial) breaks in which we check the news, (un)load the washing machine, answer a few (work?) mail or calls, plan our next holiday and do some online shopping! We are multitasking all the time, in our efforts to achieve our "must-do's" and "want-to-do's" in as short a time as possible. And at the same time, we are all complaining about how busy we all are.

Not being able to say "No!" is often provided as a reason for why we all are so busy. But is that true? And if yes, then who should we say No! to? To all others? Or... perhaps... maybe... to ourselves?

Happy reading!

Warmest regards,

Denny

Denny Portier-Terpstra
Managing Editor Amarantine

How do you say NO?

by
Norwyn Kam

It's easy... You don't.

Now let's have a deep dive into the "art of saying no" and why you should never say no to someone and see it from a different perspective. Think about the last time someone told you "no" for something that you asked or wanted. Do you remember how that felt? I can be certain that you do remember it because we were designed to remember it. Don't be confused, let me explain.

Let's go back millions of years ago in times of the cavemen, our ancestors, our origins. Life, as you know, was incredibly different. The main concern for the homo-sapiens at that moment in time was the ever-present danger that existed all around them. They were always on high alert to focus on that saber tooth tiger waiting around the corner, or where food was going to come from. Places of settlement were ever-changing, and danger was the word of the day, all day, every day. The brain thus had to adapt to these dangers and always be on alert for them. Not an easy time to live, as you can imagine, but that was the reality of human life back then. Safety was one of the most significant concerns to our distant relatives.

The human brain over the millions of years since has not changed its fundamental design and even now, in 2018, still have very primitive brains. Brains designed to keep us safe, not keep us happy. That is also why you will always remember something negative four times more, than something positive. Because when you are working with equipment that was designed to look for danger, threats, and bad circumstances, then, of course, our brains are going to be on active alert for negativity.

6

Obviously we are not living in a time that has us fearing for saber tooth tigers anymore, but that "threat" that used to be there has just changed form and now presents itself in other ways. We now perceive danger as people who don't agree with our views, people who confront us about what we say or the concern that nobody is going to like the selfie we just posted on Instagram. These are all modern day "threats" that exist, and the brain functions in the same way; looking out for these things all the time. And that's what puts us on alert, and the walls go up. Our brains are trying to protect us from negativity, and yet almost paradoxically it's designed to only look out for negativity.

And guess what is perceived as negativity? Yep, you guessed it. The feeling of being told "No" and for that reason, I'm sure that we probably all remember a time when we were told "No". Don't be too hard on yourself though; it's not that you are dwelling on it. It's just now understanding our hardwiring and why we focus on negativity more often than positive. So the next time your boss chews you up about the one wrong thing you did, when in fact you did one hundred other things right, just understand that your boss is pretty much still a Neanderthal in a suit. Still working with the same primitive brains as they did millions of years ago.

Okay but that serves as a little history on why "no" is remembered. What about not ever saying no as the title points out? So, I needed to give you a bit of the background, for you to grasp the next point. Now that you understand how "no" makes someone feel, it's understandable to see how the next person you say no to, may remember that bitterness for a long time. That may not be beneficial to you or the relationship you have with that person. People are funny creatures that can hold a silent grudge that way. Instead of saying no, there are other methods that can be used, other than the "no."

Try to ask questions instead. My experience as a certified consciousness coach has taught me many things, greatest of all is the ability to understand how powerful questions are. When you ask someone a question, it allows them the chance to see the flaws in their logic. That's how you win an argument, by the way. There's a little gift for you to try with your partner or work colleague next time. You see, the right type of questions allow someone to search their conviction and rather look for perspective. When someone has to question their stance on something, they have no choice but to think more broadly about what they believe. Most people find out that their argument is not as valid as they thought it would be, while going through this process. This can work for the "no" concept too. Let me give you an example:

> John: "Mary can you work on this urgent report for me? I need to have it done in an hour."

> Mary: "John, what will happen if this report is not done by the hour deadline you mentioned?"

> John: "Then I will have to answer to the CEO as we won't be able to fulfill our promise to our client."

> Mary: "What could you acknowledge about this

situation that you're in right now?"

John: "Well that this happens all the time. I feel that I find myself in this position every month."

Mary: "Okay, so is there something you could let go of now that you have acknowledged this?"

John: "I guess I could let go of trying to do too much and allow myself to get this worked up all the time. Our big boss is more concerned about getting out quality work anyways. He isn't too concerned on always being on time if the quality sucks."

Mary: "So what can you do differently moving forward?"

John: "I think I could plan and delegate a little earlier in the month so this doesn't happen all the time."

Do you see how in this hypothetical situation, by asking questions Mary was able to allow John to see the flaws in his logic in his request of her. She could have just said no, but instead, she used questions, not only to (politely) say no, but also to guide John into a better situation for him in the long run. I always find that questions are the best way to saying no to someone in the most beneficial way that serves both parties.

Now, I understand that this may not work all the time, and in the moments when saying no is not an option, you can always throw in a "but". Just to be clear; that's not the twerking device that you have and that you use to dance in privacy (butt). It's the word "but". By saying to someone "no, but...", what you are doing is giving someone options. And who doesn't like options? We all do. So if you can give someone an option that goes on the business end of your "no" then it doesn't have the same negative effect. Mary could have said "No John I can't do that for you, BUT I know that Jeremy has been looking for new projects to work on, so I think he would be happy to assist". Mary gave John options even though she said no. The word "but" thrown in there really takes the edge off of the no.

So give it a shot my friends. Go out there and use this information at will. Throw a few "buts" around. You know what I mean ;)

Norwyn Kam
© 2018 Norwyn Kam

Wake Pray Slay
Slaying an Unfulfilled Existence

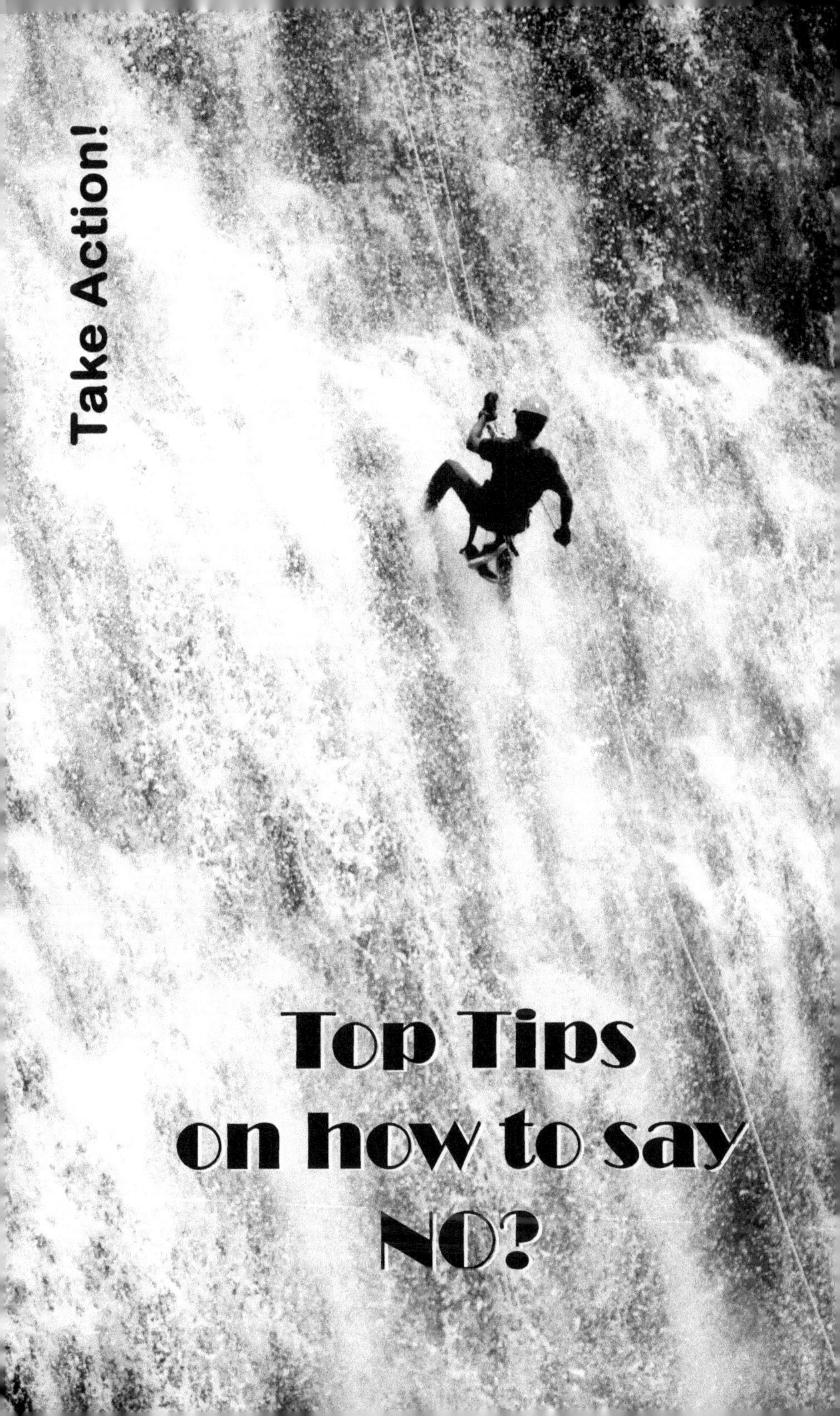
Take Action!
Top Tips on how to say NO?

"'No'
is a complete sentence".
Anne Lamott

It's hard to believe but 'no' is one of the most used words in the English language. As a two-letter word, 'no' is easy to spell, easy to pronounce, easy to understand, a complete sentence, a declaration, and can be said to be an exercise in understanding what you do not want.

So why do we all find it so hard to say? Or easy to say?

It is easy to say when a child asks a parent if they can have or do something and the parent's automatic response is 'no'. Are parents saying 'no' because they are drawing real and important boundaries. Or are they saying 'no' out of fear? Or are they saying 'no' because it's a habit?

It is more difficult to say 'no' when someone else asks you to do something for them. Often 'yes' is said out of obligation, or because you feel that someone else needs you or trusts you.

And when we do say 'no', why do we feel we have to explain our reasons?

Over the years you may have found it easier to say 'no' to your children and more difficult to say 'no' to others.

1. **What are your internal beliefs in relation to your history of saying 'yes'?**
    Opening up your journal, or taking a clean piece of paper, create three columns – the middle column headed 'yes' and the right hand column

headed 'no. In the left hand column, write down the names of every person involved in your life; whether a close relative or a distant acquaintance, write their name down. Without thinking about how to answer this next question, look at each person's name and put a tick in the column to indicate whether you more normally say 'yes' or 'no' to them.

2.   **What is the reason?**
Once you have completed step 1, then look at the 'yes' column and ask yourself, why do you more normally say 'yes' to them. Do the same for the 'no' column.

3.   **Patterns**
When you look at the people you normally say 'yes' to and the reason(s) for doing so, you will find a pattern. This pattern is often based on your own internal beliefs.

For example, you may often say 'yes' to an elderly neighbour because your parents always told you to 'respect your elders'; or you may find yourself saying 'no' to your children because your parents always said 'no' to you.

4.   **How do you say goodbye to the time vampires?**
In your list above, you will have people you normally say 'yes' to, who could also be considered to be people who take advantage of your good nature by constantly needing **your** help. They may be your nearest and dearest, or they may not be, but who are they? Who is taking

up your valuable time, when they don't need to be?

5. **Why do you not put your own life first?**
    Oooh! A question that many coaches ask their clients; the response to which often provides a huge number of reasons or excuses. If you want to say 'no', why don't you?

    These are both good questions and are often responded to with internal beliefs about how you view your relationship with other people. Write down what you have to do to be able to put your life first; as a priority to saying 'yes' to everyone else?

6. **How do you make time to say 'yes' to yourself?**
    There are no doubt a million and one things that you would like to be doing, but don't have time for. When you consider how much time you say 'yes' to others, when you would rather say 'no'; how do you start putting your own life first and say 'no' to them and 'yes' to you?

7. **Experiment!**
    'No' is a complete sentence and does not require justification or explanation; and there a huge number of ways to say 'no'. Albert Mehrabian determined that successful communication comprises of three elements – Your body language, your tone of voice, and the word(s) you use. If you are physically with someone then your body language is the greatest part of your communication; whereas in an audio only

conversation your tone of voice is the greatest part of your communication. The word(s) you use is the least important part of your communication, unless you are of course communicating in just writing. Communicating with emotion – passionately, quietly, angrily, frustrated, fearfully, etc. – has a huge impact on the way that the person/people you are talking to will interpret what you say. Your tone of voice (38% of successful communication) can demonstrate your belief in yourself, your warmth, your expertise, your support, or any other attribute that you want to demonstrate when you say 'no'. Although body language (55% of successful communication) can be communicated through a telephone, it is important that you consider when you are saying 'no' that you are congruent all the way your communication.

Try standing in front of a full length mirror and saying 'no'! See how you look. Hear how you sound. The more you experiment, the stronger you will get in your own belief of saying 'no'.

**"Don't waste your time with explanations, people only hear what they want to hear".
Paulo Coelho**

Moving into your future, these are the top tips on how to say 'no':

1. **Be clear about your own vision** and on what you want to say 'yes' to. Everything else is 'no'.

2. **Understand the implications of saying 'yes'.**

    When you really want to say 'no', saying 'yes' will take you away from your own vision and your own life plans.

3. **'No' is a complete sentence.**
    It is gratifying to say 'no' without justification and explanation.

4. **Be respectful.**
    Use the appropriate body language and tone of voice.

5. **Think before you speak.**
    Often 'yes' is the automatic response without any thought being given. Take time and think through the question or the request. How does this fit into your own vision? Then respond appropriately.

6. **No response is also a reply.**

> **"Action is the foundational key to all success".**
> **Pablo Picasso**

Step-by-Step Series

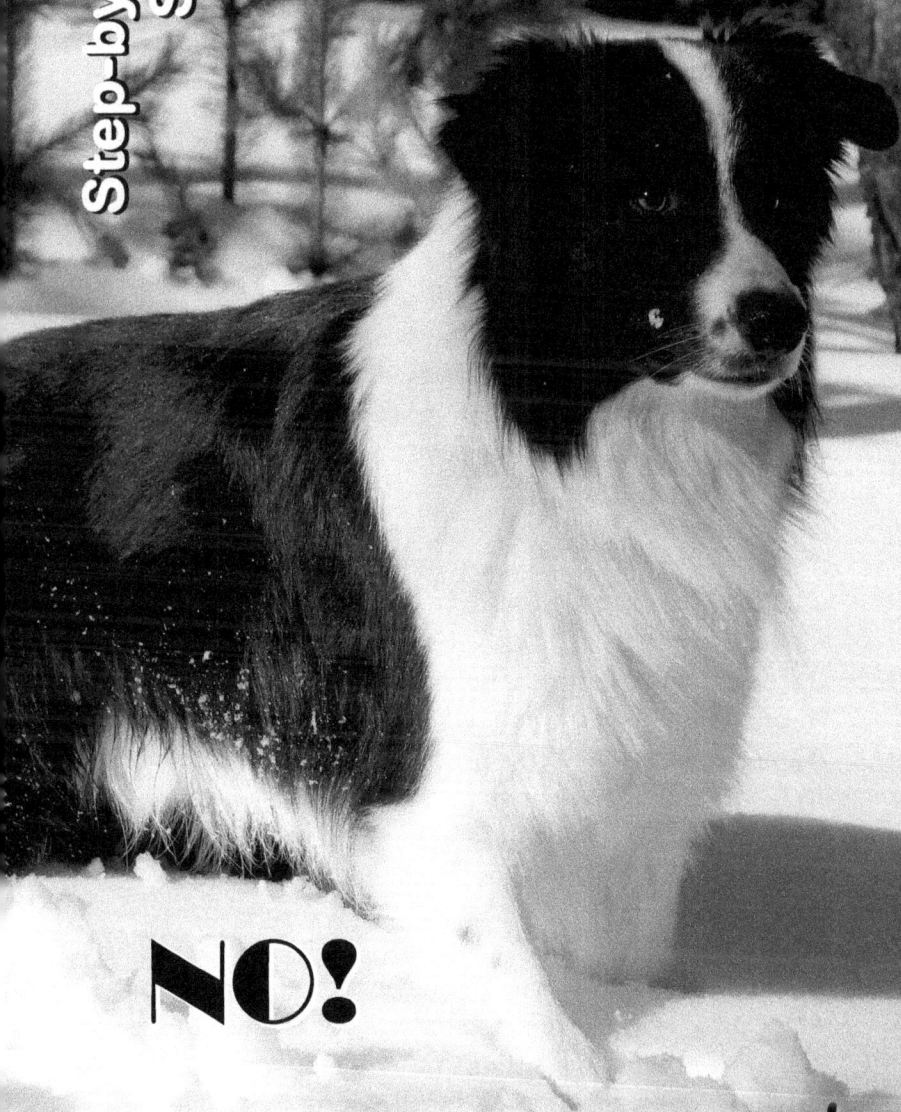

NO!

by
Barbara J. Cormack

"We must say 'no' to what, in our heart, we don't want.
We must say 'no' to doing things out of obligation,
thereby cheating those important to us of the
purest expression of our love.
We must say 'no' to treating ourselves, our health,
our needs as not as important as someone else's.
We must say 'no'".
Suzette R. Hinton

Even with only two letters, it is the hardest word in the English language to say. We say 'yes' out of obligation. Obligation not only to others but sometimes because of others. There are a lot of times and places when we should say 'no' and it often starts with us saying 'no' to ourselves first; before we learn to say 'no' to others. It's very easy to say 'yes' to ourselves because we want to live an easier life.

I recently had a wonderful experience of saying 'no' to a situation. I noticed that our 2-year old Border Collie was limping quite badly. Our vet's practice is a farming practice and is great with the 'normal day-to-day' needs of our animals, so when we took her there to be examined. As no-one in the practice could provide a clear explanation, I had to insist that we get an X-ray done. Even my partner, who had seen her limping, questioned me. I still said 'no'; there has to be a reason. I want an X-ray of her hip.

As our vets practice does not have the equipment for family pets, we were referred to local vet practice to get the X-ray. I remember sitting in the reception while she was being x-rayed, thinking 'Am I wrong in asking for this?' 'Is this unnecessary expense?'

I was doubting my intuition, my inner most feelings, which said that we needed to have her hip X-rayed. All my doubts were there because I was thinking of what the vet had said – who was I to know better?

I could have cried when I saw the results and yes, her hip was out of place.

The vet who did the X-ray told us to give her 2 months bed rest – a 2-year-old Border Collie, bed rest, really? For a dog who is used to running around 2 acres, we started taking her for walks on the lead and she was not impressed. Her 'bed rest' lasted a little longer as towards the end of the prescribed 2 months, we took a trip abroad.

Upon our return, we visited our own vet's practice again. The vets in the practice had come to the conclusion that it was a hereditary problem that we would need to manage for the rest of her life. From their knowledge and discussion with the vet who did the X-ray; it was felt that there was nothing more that we could do. Knowing the history of our Border Collie (and her dog family), I didn't understand their statement. We had previously been referred to a specialist vet; and again feeling the 'no', I asked for a referral to the specialist vet – about an hour away from us.

Although our vets practice provided the referral, they could not understand why I was asking. Again the feeling of doubt – who was I to know more than they did? I wondered for the next few days if I was wrong. Why were all these people, who knew a lot more about the topic than I did, saying something different? In my heart of hearts, I knew that I had to progress every avenue.

We arrived at the specialist vet and, very quickly after looking at the original X-ray, the specialist vet said 'It's a trauma and we can operate. It will take about three to four months and she will be back to normal.' I wanted to cry! All the worries, all the concerns about saying 'no' to everyone else, it just overwhelmed me. By listening to my inner most feelings and knowing that 'I was right!'. It wasn't a cause for celebration, but a confirmation that when you feel that you should say 'no', you must say 'no'.

After her operation, I spent time helping her to recover and learn to walk (and run) on three legs. Three weeks later we were back at our vets practice for her monthly appointment. Looking for guidance on what else I could do to help her progress to walking and running on four legs, I asked the question. One of the more experienced vets told me that she would always walk and run on three legs. NO! went through my mind. Another (younger and less experienced) vet said 'She has lost her muscle mass; it needs to be built up again'. At last, something I could focus on.

While appreciating that our vet's practice didn't have the domestic pet experience, I felt now that the goal I had set, to get her walking on all four legs before her next check-up with the specialist vet; could happen. So, I changed our daily routine to focus on helping her build up her muscle mass. As I am writing this another milestone has been reached ... and YES she is walking on all four legs. As someone who advocates a step-by-step approach to successfully achieving a goal, I know that the next step will be helping her to trot and run on all four legs.

Sometimes it is about saying 'no' to yourself; other times it is about saying 'no' to someone you love, you hold very dear to your heart; but often it about saying 'no' to someone else out of obligation to them. Saying 'no' is not always about saying 'no' to someone else, it is also about sometimes saying 'no' to yourself. What I've also learnt is that sometimes it is about being strong enough to say 'no', when you truly in your inner most heart feel 'no'.

In the last issue of Amarantine, I talked about really understanding your Wheel of Life (an umbrella view of where your life is today); taking into consideration where your life is today and from your inner most being, be absolutely clear about what you want from your life, as well as being absolutely clear about what you do not want in your life.

"Say 'no' to everything,
so you can say 'yes' to the one thing."
Richie Norton

Go back to your Wheel of Life and work through each short sentence about what your inner most heart wants from each segment of your life. Mahatma Gandhi said "Be the change you want to see in the world." When you are working through each one of your short sentences, ask yourself "Is this the change I want to see in my world?"

If your answer is 'no', then ask yourself:
- Who wants me to make this change?
- Why is this change included in my Wheel of Life?

✦   How does this change impact my world?

Change is all about exchanging one thing for another. If you are making this change for yourself, then you should include it. If you are making this change because someone else has told you to, or says that you should; you need to agree that it is included because you want to make the change and not because someone else has told you to.

One of the things that you should value is your life, and in valuing your life you should value your time. Change takes time. So, if the short sentence you have included reduces the value you have placed on your life, then say 'no'. If your inner most heart tells you 'no', then say 'no'. If it increases the value you have placed on your life, then say 'yes'.

> "People too often tend to forget that it is your own choice how you want to spend the rest of your life."
> Rachel Wolchin

If you can't say 'no' to the things or circumstances or situations or people you don't want in your life, who will?

Barbara J. Cormack
© 2018 Barbara J. Cormack

Barbara J. Cormack AFC, AFM, MNMC is an award winning coach, an author, mentor, trainer, and a sought after international speaker.

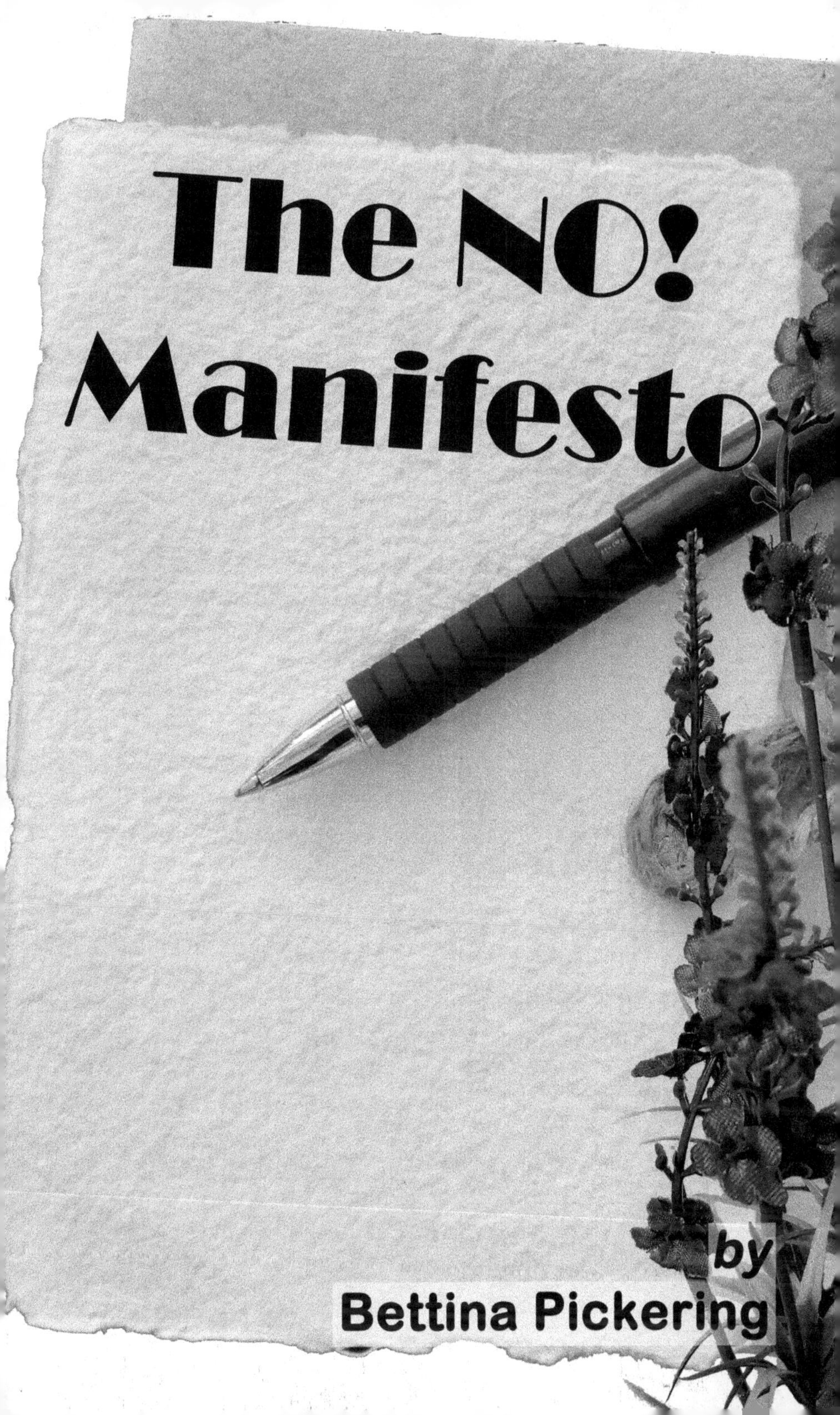
The NO!
Manifesto
by
Bettina Pickering

If you are like me and so many others suffering from boundary issues, which really means, having difficulty saying No! to anything or anyone, the No! manifesto will be your salvation.

Not being able to say No! costs. A lot.

If you are a predominant Yes! person, you will be able to recognise some or maybe all of the main consequences:

- Too little me time
- Exhaustion and tiredness
- Frustration
- Feeling under constant pressure from having to deliver, yet the list does not seem to get smaller
- Never being able to relax
- Resentment that others never do anything for me
- Always supporting other people's dreams, but not making many inroads towards your own
- Not even having clarity on your own goals and dreams
- Piling on the pounds
- Feeling overwhelmed on a regular basis
- Low self-esteem
- Your health and/or fitness suffering

What to do?

I found, just deciding to not say Yes! often does not work. The automatic nodding or jumping into the gap after being asked for help is so ingrained that we only notice when it has already happened. Deciding to say No! more often also does not work for many people. Why? Because it is too vague. In the moment when we are asked, it takes too long to go through a decision process, be firm with oneself and have a friendly answer for the help requester.

So what can we do?

Draw up the **No! Manifesto.**

A No! Manifesto – what the <bleep> is that?

A manifesto* is "a public declaration of intentions, opinions, objectives, or motives, as one issued by a government, sovereign, or organization. (*Source: dictionary.com).

You are your own sovereign, your own supreme ruler, king or queen, who can make decisions that pertain to you. No one else can make those decisions for you. This type of manifesto also works beautifully for businesses that overpromise or over give so their capacity to deliver well is overstretched.

A No! Manifesto is your declaration to the world and most importantly to YOURSELF of what you are 100% no longer doing, accepting or even considering doing. It is a powerful tool to free up time for yourself, get out of overwhelm and leave low self-esteem behind. It will help you to become confident in who you are, what you can achieve and help you turn your dreams that you keep postponing into reality.

No! MANIFESTO

for _____

I, _____, on this day __/__/__ declare:

From now on, I choose to _____

_____

_____

I say NO! to:	I say YES! to:
✗ .	✓ .
✗ .	✓ .
✗ .	✓ .
✗ .	✓ .
✗ .	✓ .
✗ .	✓ .
✗ .	✓ .
✗ .	✓ .
✗ .	✓ .
✗ .	✓ .
✗ .	✓ .
✗ .	✓ .
✗ .	✓ .
✗ .	✓ .

I know I am succeeding when I notice the following:

_____

_____

Signature: _____ Date: __/__/__

The 5 steps to drawing up your No! Manifesto

Step 1: Set your Intention

As with every manifesto first you need to declare your intent. What is your key intention that should go to the top of your manifesto?

As an example, you could put something like:

> I declare, that from now on, the xx date of xx year, I put my wellbeing first.

> Or

> I declare, that from now on, the xx date of xx year, I choose to show up as a leader.

Make sure that your declaration is positive and does NOT contain a NOT. Avoiding something does not really work when used as intention.

Once you have crafted your declaration, stand up and read it aloud as if you are stood on a stage in front of a stadium full of people. Imagine the people who matter most to you cheering you on from the front rows.

Step 2: Draw up your current habits you want to say No! to

"The difference between successful people and really successful people is that really successful people say no to almost everything." — Warren Buffett

This step is super important to get right. Your No! statements need to be phrased positively, and in the past tense. Here you identify those behaviours and habits you want to stop doing, so that you'll recognise these when they are about to happen.

Make sure you include what these behaviours or habits result in, or in other words what effect they have on you.

Examples might be:

- When a friend or colleague asks me to help them out, I tended to say yes without first checking my diary or my other commitments to myself.
- I packed my day so full that I feel overwhelmed and a non-achiever when something unexpected happens.
- I didn't take enough time for myself in the day / the week, and feel depleted at the end of the week.

You can of course write down as many as you like. I would recommend you start with 3-5 of your main ones, or if there is one that is huge, stick to one. Less is more on this occasion.

Step 3: Draw up your Yes's, this is what I will do instead

Now that you have identified those behaviours that don't serve you and their results, you can create your Yes!, this is what I will do instead behaviours.

These might look like:

No!, this behaviour does not serve me	Yes!, this is what I will do instead
✗ When a friend or colleague asks me to help them out, I tended to say yes without first checking my diary or my other commitments to myself. ✗ I packed my day so full that I feel overwhelmed and a non-achiever when something unexpected happens. ✗ I didn't take enough time for myself in the day / the week, and feel depleted at the end of the week.	✓ When someone asks me to do something new, I take a breath, respond that I will check my commitments, and get back to them with an answer in the next day or so. Only if this is truly something that supports my goals or I really want to do will I say YES to it. ✓ I only schedule 50% of time each day with to do's or meetings. The other time I spend preparing for the next day and/or actioning meetings ✓ I commit to scheduling at least 1 hour a day of me time. I do things that I enjoy.

Know that your Yes! behaviours do not need to correspond to your No! behaviours one to one. You can have 3 No! behaviours that are covered by one Yes! behaviours. The key thing is that you have a Yes! behaviour that can replace the No! behaviour(s).

Habits take time to change. You can speed up that time and change them fast by tackling one first, then once that has become a positive habit, the next and so on. It is so much easier and effortless to change one thing, than several.

Step 4: Measuring your success

Track the success of your No! Manifesto, daily. You decide what lets you know that you are well on the way to success.

Write your measures down on your No! Manifesto.

I know I am succeeding when I notice the following:

- I feel calm and in control,
- I feel excited and happy,
- I get 100% of my daily list done,
- I have 1 hour free for myself each day.

Examples of cool tracking mechanisms are:

- ***Smile board:***

- *Feelings Odometer:*

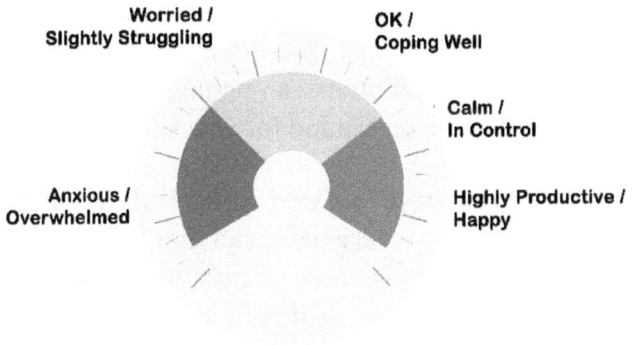

- ## Counting your No!'s vs Yes!'s

  Give yourself a badge, a tick or a small coin ($0.10, £0.10 or €0.10) for each time you act on your No! and Yes! statements on your No! Manifesto.

There are loads of other options. Get creative and find the measures and a mechanism that works for you.

The most important thing is: IT MUST BE FUN!

Step 5: Re-inforce your No! Manifesto every day

Finally Sign your No! Manifesto, and date it with today's date. This is crucial. You are making a real commitment to yourself and others, so signing it physically with a pen is part of taking a stand for yourself.

Now you have created your No! Manifesto hang it somewhere where you can easily see it and see it regularly. Ideally, in eye height when you stand in front of it. What works well is to stick it on a door that you open and close frequently.

Each time you wish to open the door on which your No! Manifesto hangs, stop and read your manifesto. Notice how your manifesto is working for you.

If you need to change anything, reflect on this and decide what to adjust. Congratulate yourself on your successes, however small. Acknowledge your efforts.

After three beautiful breaths and a genuine smile, open the door and walk through it.

Bettina Pickering
© 2018 Bettina Pickering

Bettina Pickering is a transformative leadership coach, entrepreneur mentor, business transformation and change consultant, author and speaker.

Resources: If you wish to download the No! Manifesto template, go to www.aronagh.com/nomanifesto

Newest Trends

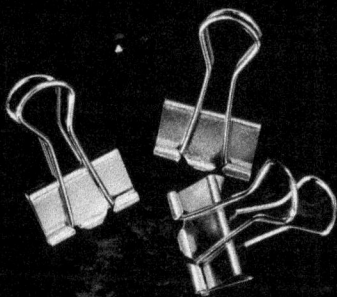

delete

HELLO DAY
DIARY 2017-2018

Whose life is it?

"The difference between successful people
and very successful people
is that very successful people say 'no'
to almost everything."
Warren Buffett (Billionaire US Investor)

Steve Jobs (1955-2011) is a classic example of how and when to say 'no'. Steve, the co-founder of Apple re-joined the company in 1997 as it was on the verge of bankruptcy.

One of the challenges we all face is the huge volume of options open and requests made to us each day; but how do you know which one to say 'yes' to and which one to say 'no' to?

Richard Branson is known for saying "If you don't have time for the small things, you won't have time for the big things." He is known as "Doctor Yes" because he believes that life is more fun when you say and grab most opportunities; but he also admits that although saying 'yes' can open up wonderful opportunities, saying 'no' is a skill that everyone should possess.

When Steve Jobs returned to Apple after an absence of twelve years, he found a huge number of different projects or options that the company was working on. Often known as the scattergun approach. So many things but not one becoming a success. He terminated a large range of projects and focused on one or two. As more ideas were brought to him, he said 'no' and continued to focus on one or two.

So how you do you say 'no'? Take 10 minutes out of your very busy day and answer these questions:

1. What would I say 'yes' to if I only have 4 weeks to live?
    -   On a scale of 1 to 10 (where 1 is unimportant and 10 is incredibly important), how important is each item on this list to my life today?

2. What is on my bucket list?
    -   On a scale of 1 to 10 (where 1 is unimportant and 10 is incredibly important), looking at my bucket list, what would happen if I didn't achieve one or more of these items?

3. What happens when I say 'yes' to something through obligation or a need to please someone else, which means that I say 'no' to something I want or want to do?

4. What happens when I say 'no' to someone else and 'yes' to me?

5. How important is my life to me?

6. If I only had my life to live, what would I focus on?

7. How do I create a life that allows me to say 'yes' when I want to and 'no' when I want to? What do I have to do?

In today's world life is busy and things are coming at you and going past you very fast. As more and more technologies get created, there are a huge number of opportunities. The complication though is that we believe we have to do it all. The reality is that we are being pulled into saying 'yes' without taking time out to THINK.

Saying 'no' is all about valuing yourself and your time; so how do you create a life that really matters to YOU? A life that allows you to say 'no' and mean it? A life that allows you to select when to say 'yes' and get involved?

"The best advice I could give anyone
is to spend your time working on whatever
you are passionate about in life."
Richard Branson

"People think focus means saying YES
to the thing you've got to focus on.
But that's not what it means at all.
Innovation is saying NO
to 1,000 good things."
Steve Jobs

"When you say YES to others,
make sure you are not saying
NO to yourself."
Paulo Coelho

"No matter
what people tell you,
words and ideas
can change the world."
Robin Williams

"Half the troubles in this life
can be traced to
saying YES to quickly
and not
saying NO soon enough."
Josh Billings

"LEARN THE ART OF SAYING NO.
Don't lie.
Don't make excuses.
Don't over-explain yourself.
Just simply decline."
Anon

"Saying NO to something
is actually more powerful
than saying YES."
Tom Hanks

"NO is a
complete sentence."
Anne Lamott

"Information overload (on all levels) is
exactly WHY you need an "ignore list".
It has never been more important
to say "NO"."
Mani S. Sivasubramanian

Saying No!

by

Alyson Daley

Why do we feel that it isn't right to use 'no' too often? Why are we afraid of the implications of saying no?

How do we say no to something that we don't want to do? Something that we don't feel comfortable with, something that doesn't align with who we truly are; how often do we go along with something when we don't want to? Let me ask you, please, take a few moments, relax, sit back & ponder, when was the last time you said okay, yes, alright then, when all you wanted to say was those two small letters that make up that word that we are all seemingly scared to say: 'no'.

Do you find yourself asking 'why did I do that, why couldn't I say no?' Could it be to keep the peace, to make them happy, to make life easier? Because if we didn't say no, what would be the consequences, the outcome, the response; and would we be able to deal with those; could it be perhaps this is why we don't say no, the trade off, the pay off, so we just carry on sacrificing ourselves.

Some reasons could be that we are a people pleaser, want to look good in the eyes of others, fear of being rejected, and fear of confrontation or its pure altruism, these are to name but a few. Which one resonates with you?

It could also be a cultural thing, for example British people generally speaking have 'the stiff upper lip mentality'. 'Put up & shut up'. Some have said it is because the British are 'too polite'. For example, if out for a meal and the waiter comes along to ask if everything is okay with our meal, we reply 'yes' literally seconds after we had said how awful it is. We say yes when we want to say no. WHY? Scared of upsetting someone? Coming across rude? Due to our own personal experience of being told no, and how being told no made us feel? Or is it innate, this feeling of saying no? Or is it cultural?

Can we unlearn what has been ingrained in us? Yes we can. This will be discussed momentarily. But I want to go down a different route first.

Our wellbeing, our Emotional, Psychological & Mental Wellbeing (EPMW); how does this relate, well, if we are off kilter with any one of those, a mix of two or all three, then saying no can wreak havoc with our equilibrium. At any point in our life we will be faced with one, two or all three of our EPMW being affected. How do we face the challenges that are presented to us; let alone saying 'NO' when the word 'no' is seemingly such a hard word to say and follow through with. It can seem like such a mountainous journey. Anxiety can take over and we become frozen with our decision-making skills. Our thoughts can run amuck, running all over the place like a Tasmanian devil. Hence, saying no becomes an even harder word to say and do.

One of the ways to help reduce this anxiety is being in the moment. Bringing our minds back to the present moment in time. How do we do that? A suggestion is to focus on your breathing, paying attention to your in-breath, hold for a few seconds and release, exhaling for as long as you can, repeating this for as long as you need; you will know when to stop as you will feel a sense of peace or relaxation. Another suggestion is, tap your feet on the floor, look at your hands, scratch your nose;

anything that is a small simple move, do it. What this does, is distract our mind even though for a short moment. Yet, that moment is long enough to then create other moments. If possible add physical activity such as

going to make a drink, walk around your office (providing it's big enough), go and talk with a fellow work colleague…; this list is endless, yet nothing too mind frazzling. If it won't make you feel good, don't do it. You know you better than anyone else; this is about getting in touch with the inner you, listening to yourself. Practise, practise, & more practise.

With this practice, your mind will ease and you will get more in touch with yourself and how you view yourself will change. This, in turn, will lift your self-esteem. Positive thoughts about how you feel about yourself will increase along with your self-worth and self-respect.

This is a prime time to think about your values, wants, needs and boundaries. What are they? Write them down, say them out loud. What are your needs? Are they being met? And what about those boundaries? Have you set any, and if so, are they being met? Has anyone crossed those boundaries, and have you allowed this to happen by not saying no?

Conversely with the practice in hand, as your self-esteem, self-respect and value of self increase, now is the time to practise saying 'no'. Let's practice and visualise what it looks like saying 'no'. Picture saying 'no' in your mind's eye. What does it feel like saying 'no'? What sounds can you hear (apart from saying 'no' haha) i.e. a running stream, birds tweeting, smells of coffee, toast or pancakes; the clothes you are wearing and most importantly how are you stood, how does that feel? Grounded from the mindfulness that you have practised, one hopes! Confident, knowing that you are speaking from a good place, love, that you are honouring yourself, valuing yourself by saying 'no'. See it in your mind's eye, play it out, feel that amazing proud feeling when you say 'no'.

And then, rub your left ear or touch your watch strap (these are suggestions, you will find one that works for you). This technique is called anchoring. Every time you want or need to say 'no', rub your left ear, your watch strap, or anyplace else that works best for you as your anchor. This will take you straight back to that empowering moment when you said 'no' before and stood by that no. It will take you back to the time when you created that anchor and felt great about saying no, and you will be able to say 'no' again. It will get easier the more you practice, the more you get in tune with you, the truer you are to yourself. When we speak and act from a place of love, we can never go wrong. This goes hand-in-hand with our self-esteem, our self-worth and personal constructs (Kelly, 1955).

Alyson Daley
© 2018 Alyson Daley

Lecturer in Psychology (University of Huddersfield and Bradford College), Huddersfield Change Project volunteer, Mental Health Practitioner, and Energy Mover

Saying NO when your heart wants to say YES ...

by

Dr Charuni Senanayake

There are lots of decisions that we are trained to take from our childhood. As a child, decision making is perhaps the easiest, as they can say 'yes' or 'no' just by considering the need of that given time. As we grow up, lots of things need to be taken into account, starting from the situation that you are in, the people involved, the occasion presented, the appropriateness, the alternatives, the cost, the time, the implications of the decision all the way to the words to be used to say it.

As a child, I had a peaceful and secure family. As I grew up, I became independent and confident, and the insecurities that I felt as a teenager reduced. I accepted myself for who I had become and I felt comfortable with it. I had no issue at all with being in a new crowd and not knowing what to say. I always did what felt good, and never at any given moment did anything that was considered as "not appropriate'. And being aware of this made made me very comfortable with the way I lived. My life was an open book.

Until one day, I met someone whom I'd never met before. As we got along, I sensed for some reason that I knew him from the past. I understood exactly how he felt and there were so many commonalities between us. I liked things, places, moments, songs and he liked those all the same. We were direct and open with each other about what we felt. As our friendship grew, our feelings grew towards boundaries that we didn't want to touch, and I knew the time had come for us to have the difficult conversation. I knew I had limits which I never dared to cross. My heart said YES but my brain said NO.

I would understand exactly how you may feel in a similar

situation, as I've been there. The values that I had developed, the principles that I had created, and the goodness towards others involved in my life took over. I, as a person, became the last to be considered. I will always question myself 'did I do the right thing?' and repeatedly I've told myself YES. Was I a coward? No, I did what I had to do, because of the people around me and because I cared a great deal about them. Regret is worse than rejection? I am yet to experience it.

There are times when saying 'No' is not easy, particularly when it's a very personal decision dear to your heart. There are no right or wrong ways to doing it, and opinions may also differ from individual to individual. When the circumstances presented secretes happy dopamine or serotonin as neurochemicals in our brain, and when your heart rate increases, it doesn't mean it should always be a YES situation. That is why you are perhaps given both a brain and a mind!

Through my experiences in life, I would like to share some of the heart-felt points that might help someone else, who might be facing a similar situation. Please consider below, prior to making that difficult decision.

1. **Know it is personalized to you:**
   Your personal situation is yours and not anyone else's. Trying to look into others who had similar issues, and how they took their decisions, may not always be applicable to you, due to uniqueness of each situation. You can consider such situations as to look at options, or ask your best buddies what to do, but do not rely only on their suggestions for a way forward. Instead look deeper into yourself 'How

would you face the situation?", "What is acceptable to you?", "What is it, that you have to have to give up in order for you to have what is in the offer?", "How prepared are you to live with the consequences?". These questions can only be answered truthfully by you and by no-one else.

I was truthful in my answers to myself, I weighed the consequences against the gains of my decision and I knew the answer right away, though I admit that it didn't register as "super right" at that time.

2. **Take time to think things through logically:**
Many things, as they become very personal to us, create heart bonds which are good. But those bonds can also blind us, especially if we only consider the shorter term of "how it can affect us". Prior to making a decision in a very personal matter, be bold and go the extra mile, take time and think through every angle. Don't be in a hurry. Have that open conversation with yourself. Think about your values, what you stand for, and how close your decision is to this. Remember, in the short run, many can live with a not-carefully-planned decision. But in the longer run, you will pay the price from your consciousness, if you didn't accept it as "right" or "wrong" when you took the decision. While allowing yourself to enjoy the beauty of your heart-felt decisions, involve your brain in thinking logically about the decision made by your heart. When you involve both your heart and brain, whatever the decision is, this will help you to "accept" it better, as well as help you to live peacefully.

I saw many opportunities including probably "could be happiest" for a short duration, if I went ahead with the situation presented and when I considered it only at a shallow level. As I considered the longer term and involved my logically thinking brain, I saw that I would never be able to accept it consciously, as I realized that my decision would've negatively affected the three people that I loved dearly and who had been in my life for a long time.

3. **Think about the consequences of a wrong decision in advance:**
You will never know the pain of living with consequences until it happens to you and you start living with them. If you violate your inner most values and principles, the consequences will follow. If your decision doesn't violate your innermost values and principles, grab the first chance of saying YES!!!

If I went ahead with an YES in the presented situation, it could have affected my children's lives in the long run. Both of my children are very attached to each other, they would have lost a happy and secure early life, and I would have felt I made a wrong decision, as it was against my own values and principles, which I held dearly.

4. **Once taken the decision, stick with it:**
Create a distance with the people and things involved in the situation for a while, until you fully accept the difficult decision. It will help you to avoid wondering 'Did I do the right thing?". Gently have the conversation with yourself until the "full" acceptance

happens internally over time. Know and understand yourself, and don't be hard on yourself. Many have done it, and lived with it, and you are not alone. Look at ways to spend your time wisely. Catch up with an old friend, do something new, pamper yourself, etc. Most people regret a negative decision for not having the courage to go ahead, but as many people regret having the courage to make a positive decision when they see how it has affected their life later on.

I will admit that it was hard at the beginning, but I kept myself busy and distracted. I knew I did the right thing, but I Googled solutions as I needed additional ways to cope with this decision. I did a lot of things not to be "too alone with myself" for periods of time. I was also not afraid to cry during moments that I felt low, but I always made sure to tell myself that it was OK to feel what I felt, and that I would soon get used to it. Time is indeed a great healer.

5. Deal with the regret of saying NO:
Everyone who says NO in a very personal matter will always have a tiny chance of regret, as we are only human. Quotes like "Always do what your heart desires" are great quotes, but they may not be applicable in each situation. You may question yourself. "Am I being a coward?". The best time to think about the answer to this question is prior to making the actual decision. If the answer is YES at that time, re-assess all answers you would have gathered including a re-check of your values and principles. Once the decision has been made and you have reached the "acceptance phase", be careful whom you choose to share these feelings with.

Inviting in the opinions of others, when you are having minor doubts about a decision that you've made, can bring more regret than the situation actually warrants.

While I'm sharing my personal experience here, there will be others who have faced similar situations, and who would have taken a more positive decision and lived happily ever after as well. But this article is written to cover situations where you need to take a decision and may feel that you have to say NO whilst your heart says YES.

Our decisions are very personal to us just like our situations are. I believe there are no right or wrong decisions, only "moments" that have created us to think of them as right or wrong due to the circumstances presented with them. Dare to be different than the usual herd, dare to challenge yourself during difficult times, dare to live with a decision which you thought was "the best" at that given time, and know that we grow by experimenting with decisions throughout our lives.

Charuni Senanayake
© 2018 Dr Charuni Senanayake

Life Coach,
Executive Coach
and
Coach Trainer

Tools, Models, Techniques

The
Art of Saying
"No"!

Richard Branson is known as "Doctor Yes" because he believes life is a lot more fun when you say 'yes'. He admits in a Virgin blog (2 June 2015) that 'yes' isn't always the most appropriate answer. He is offered business ideas and opportunities regularly and he goes on to say that 'while saying yes opens up doors to wonderful possibilities, knowing when to say no is a skill that everyone should possess.'

While kitesurfer Nick Jacobsen was able to say 'no' to jumping off from Moskito Island; Richard got caught up in peer pressure and made his jump in the dark and windy weather when launching Virgin America's at the Palms in Las Vegas.

Although he knew he should go back inside, take off the harness and tell everyone that the jump should be postponed; he allowed himself to be encouraged to jump and was left feeling 'like a rag doll hanging there dripping blood, in front of a party of Virgin America guests'; when he was blown into the side of the building on his way down.

He ends this blog with 'Yes is best, but no can be smart too. Go with your gut, trust your instincts, and don't let others sway your opinion. If you need to, just say no!'

When Steve Jobs returned to Apple in 1997, one of his first strategic moves was to say 'no'.

Apple was losing money, struggling to survive, and had taken the decision to produce as many different products as possible, with as many different marketing ideas, in the hope that one would capture the imagination of their consumers.

His decision to say 'no' to as many good products and marketing ideas as possible, was to allow the company to focus its limited resources on a few great products that he believed the consumers would purchase.

Although the benefits of saying 'no' are well documented, many people, including successful business leaders, struggle to say 'no'.

Steve Job's ability to say 'no' repeatedly allowed Apple to develop the iconic iMacs, from which other products followed.

When has saying 'no' been the right decision for you?

John Kenneth Galbraith, a Canadian-born economist, public official, and confident of US President Lyndon Johnson. In his autobiography, *A life in our times,* Galbraith wrote about an experience of saying 'no'.

He was tired after a rough schedule and asked his housekeeper, Emily Gloria Wilson (long standing member of his staff), to hold any telephone calls while he took a nap.

The telephone rang. "Lyndon Johnson here. Get me Ken Galbraith. I want to talk to him."

Emily said "He's resting, Mr. President."

"Well, get him up. I need to talk to him."

Emily responded "No, I'm sorry, I can't. I work for him, not for you, Mr. President" and she put down the phone.

When Galbraith awoke and was told that the President had called, he was mortified that the President had been kept waiting.

Galbraith immediately called the President to apologise, but was surprised when the President said "Tell that woman I want her here in the White House!"

Research

NO

Saying no has a lot to do with being assertive, as opposed to being under-assertive or over-assertive (a.k.a. "aggressive). Where being under-assertive is seen as typical female behaviour, being over-assertive is seen as typically male. The difference between the two usually relates back to the value that we place on either achieving a desired outcome (over-assertive and male) or on the relationship that we have with the other (under-assertive and female).

Assertiveness is the middle ground; we want to achieve the desired outcome for ourselves, without negatively impacting our relationship with the other(s), and therefore we are respectful towards the (wants, needs and feelings of) the other(s) too.

Not being assertive is usually led by strong emotions, such as fear (of damaging the relationship or not getting the desired outcome), insecurity (not being sure about how your own needs and feelings matter too) or even anger (wanting the desired outcome at any expense and really not caring about the other(s)). So, you may think that we can always be assertive, if we simply don't allow our own emotions to hinder our behaviour.

Unfortunately, that's not true. Behaviour can be perceived differently in different situations. Where in the Middle East walking away from negotiations may be part of everyday business, in most of the Western world people will perceive that to be rude. When an always helpful person says no that may come as a shock, whilst nobody would expect anything else from someone who says no all the time. And then there is the perception of assertiveness in itself too. Research carried out amongst professional negotiators showed that in only about 50% of the cases, the sending and receiving party agreed to which extend the behaviour shown would qualify as being under-assertive, assertive or over-assertive!

Should we then perhaps abandon the principles of assertiveness altogether, and just struggle on like we've always done? Well, yes and no. I think it's important that we all understand that "being assertive" is something that nobody will always be 100% successful at. So don't get frustrated when you feel you've failed, you simply can't win them all. Having said that, as assertiveness has proven to be the best way to pursuit our goals in harmony with the people around us, I think it's definitely worth the effort of at least trying to be as assertive as you possibly can.

But how can you do that? That's actually quite simple, when you keep in mind that we should always be respectful towards the wants, needs and feelings of yourself and of the other(s).

Start by taking yourself seriously. A well-known script for starting an assertive conversation, is the **DESC-scirpt**, which goes as follows:

> **D**escribe the situation objectively
> *"The last time we drove to town, we took my car".*
>
> **E**xpress your own feelings (and use "I" instead of "you")
> *"I don't mind driving, but I'd like to have a drink*

every now and then too".

Specify the desired outcome
"I would like us to rotate who's driving".

List the **C**onsequences
"so that we can take turns driving each other home safely, and enjoying a drink whilst we are out".

And then move on to take the other(s) seriously too. Being respectful is not about giving in, but it is about ensuring that the other party knows that you've heard them, listened to them, and that you've taken their points into account too. Listen to what the other is telling you, repeat it to show that you've heard and that you've understood it, and by doing so acknowledge that the other and their wants, needs and feelings are important to you as well. And then check back in with your own desired outcome, to ensure that you don't forget about yourself in the conversation.

Write it down if you have to, and consciously make a decision to stick to your gums, give in, or find a compromise. When you simply start with sharing and listening, you will be in a very good place to become a trained and skilled assertive!

https://www.researchgate.net/publication/318146012_Interpersonal_assertiveness_Inside_the_balancing_act

It's all in the Numbers

Numbers

Introduction

by
Loren Schmal

For anyone who is interested, curious or even a true believer, the basic definition of numerology is the universal language of numbers. By breaking down the patterns of the universe into numbers, we are able to uncover information about the world as a whole, as well as every individual. Numerology is the science of numbers, but it only involves simple mathematics.

It's more about the personalities of each number, and how each numbers' traits alter the course of your life depending on where they appear in your personal Numerology - if they appear at all. Numerology is a tool used to investigate our own very being, and to bring light our highest potential on the physical, emotional, mental and spiritual planes. Numerology tells of our potential destiny, our natural talents and helps us gain a better understanding of ourselves and others. It shows us the pathway we need to take in our lives to fulfill this potential, and also, tells us one of the many reasons why each one has different traits and characteristics. Numbers have been in existence since the beginning of time and predates all Alphabets.

Each number has a different vibration, and can therefore give us a better understanding of one's pathway, and the circumstances which surround our life. It can direct one to the career best suited to each person, and gives us the opportunity to be more aware of the talents we have and of the pathways we choose to utilize them. It also tells us of the compatibility we have with another, especially who would be most compatible as a partner for you. It tells you how you may best help your family and friends, due to the numbers which control their lives.

Each number is influenced by a different planet in our Solar System. Each letter of the alphabet vibrates to a given number, 1 – 9, which is also the span of our life cycles. The numbers under which we were born, plus the numbers in our names, are the tools that we are given in order that we may accomplish our mission in life, and enable us to work through all our Karmic Lessons. The Vibratory Power of each number affects us in both Positive and Negative ways.

HOW TO WORK OUT
YOUR OWN NUMEROLOGY

The symbolic meanings that surround the nine whole numbers are the centre of Numerological divination. Numbers are also keyed to letters of the alphabet, so words and names, as well as dates of birth, can be analysed.

Numerology in
Relation to the Alphabet

Each letter of the alphabet is represented by a number between 1 and 9.

1	–	A	J	S
2	–	B	K	T
3	–	C	L	U
4	–	D	M	V
5	–	E	N	W
6	–	F	O	X
7	–	G	P	Y
8	–	H	Q	Z
9	–	I	R	

NAME NUMEROLOGY

The First Name is our 'Foundation in Life'.

To find the total Numerological vibration of your name, translate the letters of your name into the numbers as listed above, and add those number together. Then, break down the result in separate numbers, which you add up again, until you have reduced it to a single digit number. This number is known as your Name Ruling Number.

As an example, let's take the name Chantel. This name translates to C=3, H=8, A=1, N=5, T=2, E=5, L=3.

When we add those numbers (3+8+1+5+2+5+3) we get to 27.

As this is a double digit, which we still need to reduce to 1 digit, we add the numbers of this result.

So: 2+7=9.

The Name Ruling Number for the name Chantel is therefore 9.

DATE OF BIRTH NUMEROLOGY

DAY NUMBER

Your Day Number is the energy which influences who you are and all that you do in your life, on a daily basis. It tells of what makes you respond and act as you do, and is an indication of what type of life you should lead in order to be successful in all that you undertake in this lifetime.

Your Day Number is the day of your birth.

Using as an example the 26th of September 1967, the Day Number is 26 = 2 + 6 = 8.

8 is the Day Number.

DESTINY NUMBER

The destiny number is one of the most important numbers on your chart. It is the ruling force that describes what you must do/learn, in order to operate harmoniously with your environment and how you can get the most out of your present life. It shows the direction you must take, representing the only opportunities for success that will be made available to you.

To analyse and interpret your 'Destiny Number', simply use the formula of reducing your entire date of birth to a single digit.

For example, the 'Destiny Number' for a person with the date of birth of the 26th of September 1967 is 2+6+0+9+1+9+6+7 = 40,
4+0 = 4.

PERSONAL YEAR

The Personal Year Number is the energy by which you will live your life from your birthday of this year, until your birthday of next year. This is the vibration that will influence all that you do throughout that period.

The Personal Year energy is present from birthday to birthday. To work out your Personal Year Number, take the Day and Month Numbers and add them to the Year Number.

For example, the Personal Year Number in 2018 for someone with the date of birth 26/09/1967 would be Number 1. Add the day and month numbers to the year number (2018)
2+6+0+9+2+0+1+8 = 28:
2 + 8 = 10:
1+0=1, making 1 the Personal Year Number.

Loren Schmal
© 2018 Loren Schmal

Founder of CyberPA

Numerology Series

It's all in the Numbers

11

by
Loren Schmal

The NUMBER 11 or 2

Welcome to 2018; a truly significant year in Numerology as it is a Master 11/2 Universal Year with the Overall Theme being LOVE!

In numerology, the Universal Year is like the landscape or terrain you're driving through all year long and is calculated by adding the numbers of the current year together. A Universal Year means that everyone on the planet will be feeling the energy related to a particular number during the entire year.

The 11/2 Universal Year

You calculate the Universal Year by simply adding the numbers in the current year (in this case, 2018) together like this:

$$2018 = 2 + 0 + 1 + 8 = 11$$
11 is a Master number

Then reduce again:

$$1 + 1 = 2$$

Some numerologists never reduce the Master numbers and so this would be an 11 Universal Year.

Other numerologists indicate the Master numbers by writing it this way:

11/2

Meet the Master Numbers
Numerology's difficult little blessings

In Numerology, every number is significant, yet there are three numbers to pay extra-special attention to: 11, 22 and 33 -- these are called "Master numbers."

These three Master numbers have profoundly powerful meanings, and when they appear in your chart, they can hint at difficulty. But Master numbers are often not well understood - they can be just as much of a curse as they can be a blessing. They give you insight into obstacles by calling upon your patience and maturity - and a lot of effort - to peacefully integrate these elements into your personality. If you, personally, can master these Master numbers in your chart, however, they can be the most powerful and productive numbers of all.

Master number 11

The number 11 represents instinct, and is the most intuitive of all numbers. It is your connection to your subconscious, to gut feeling and knowledge without rationality. Because the 11 has all the qualities of the 2 (since 1 + 1 = 2), the negative points of the 11 - anxiety, shyness, stressed energy - are balanced out by the 2's qualities of charisma and inspiration. 11 is the dichotomy number, meaning it is both extremely conflicted and also a dynamic catalyst.

The danger of the 11 is that it needs to be focused on a very specific, concrete goal. If you have 11 in your chart and it isn't attached to a specific project, you will most likely experience anxiety and fear. It's extremely powerful and capable of great things, but can also be extremely self-sabotaging when not used correctly.

If you have the Master number 11 in your Numerology chart, tap into it and use it to create personal power and spiritual evolution. Do not deny your instincts, and let your inner, guiding voice push you toward growth and stability. This is a number of faith, and very much associated with psychics, clairvoyants and prophets.

Master number 22

The Master number 22 holds more power than any other number (earning it the nickname "the Master Builder"). It is a pragmatic number, a doer, capable of spinning wild dreams into concrete reality. Those who have 22 in their Numerology chart have great potential for success. That's because it has all the intuition of the number 11, paired with a grounded and scientific approach associated with the number 4 (because 2 + 2 = 4). 22 is an ambitious but disciplined number.

The 22 represents lofty goals brought down to earth and made into something you can touch. It is a grandiose thinker with great confidence and leadership qualities. Unfortunately, not everyone with a 22 in their chart is practical. This is symbolized by the brilliant person you might know, who doesn't "live up to" their potential. This is the danger of both the 11 and 22; though both are capable of greatness, they can shy away from great opportunities or apply too much pressure on themselves.

If you have 22 in your chart, ease up and realize your limitless opportunities. Turn down the pressure-cooker and realize your shot at serving the world in an effective and practical way.

Master number 33

The 33 is the mover and shaker of the Master numbers (earning it the nickname "Master Teacher"). With 11 and 22 combined in this Master number, intuition and dreams reach an entirely new orbit. A 33 used to its full potential means that there is no personal agenda, only a focus on humanitarian issues. Someone with 33 strongly featured in their chart has the ability to throw themselves into a project that goes far beyond mere practicality.

The number 33 represents full understanding before communication. With 33 represented in one's Numerology chart, that person is probably highly knowledgeable, but also fact-checks before preaching ideas or ideals.

This number in full efficiency is a sight to behold. But this is rare. Master number 33 is only significant if it's one of your Core numbers -- Life Path, Heart's Desire, Personal Expression, Personality or Maturity numbers. Otherwise, Numerology experts look at 33 as simply 6 (or 33/6, still weakening its power and downgrading it from a Master number).

Numerology experts pay special attention to Master numbers, and you should too. The best way to consider them? That 11, 22 and 33 create a triangle of enlightenment.

What Do You Need to Know About The 11/2 Universal Year?

The power of the Master numbers resides in its inherent polarity. With the 11, the repeated number 1 can be considered a masculine energy adding to the number 2, which can also be considered a feminine energy. This energetic matrix holds immeasurable power with the potential of the convergence of the most optimal qualities of the blending of masculine and feminine energy.

The Master number brings with it an intensity that's undeniable. It's generally observed that the Master numbers bring a higher spiritual purpose, no matter how you might define that. The Master numbers carry a higher frequency and vibratory influence. In practical terms, the year 2018 is a year where the energy supporting and guiding all of us is rather intense. This means that we're going to feel high-strung mixed with a certain level of anxiety. We're going to feel a constant push and pull to be more and do better, often to the point of distraction. You might also notice that you have higher expectations for yourself, even when others can't see that those feelings are going on inside of you. Everyone will be getting the internal call to step it up this year.

So what does that mean for you on a practical level? It means that we're here to "master" the elements presented to us within the frequency, vibration, and "theme" presented by the Master 11. It means that our strengths will be bolstered and yet we'll also be faced with more significant challenges. The bottom line: It's not easy! Master numbers not only demand that we step up and take the lead in life, they also make conflicting demands on us. The Master Numbers are innately in conflict with themselves.

Take the Master number 11 as an example. The 11 is a double on; all about the self, creativity, initiation, independence, innovation, and self-confidence. Yet the foundational energy for the 11 is the 2, which is all about others, partnership, group dynamics, being supportive, and behind the scenes. So can you see how we can feel conflicted and potentially confused when dealing with the energy presented by the 11? Working with Master numbers is a marathon, not a sprint. This year in particular, we must train, be flexible, pace ourselves, and invest in the right equipment.

We're also being schooled in developing and acting with humility. The Master numbers always bring certain heightened levels of ego to the game. Therefore, we'll be on the fast track to learning how to level and soften the ego without sublimating our superior gifts. We must connect with a sincere and deep sense of humility before we can manifest and harness the power of the Master number.

Get ready for a year of spiritual illumination! The most important concept to grasp is that the Master number 11 is the spiritual messenger. The Master numbers carry a higher frequency, vibration, and spiritual purpose. Energetically speaking, they're always pushing us into a higher form of self-realization and self-actualization. A Master number demands expansion and evolution, yet expansion and evolution most often take place within, or in response to, severe or intensified circumstances. The key is to understand what the foundational energy of the 2 brings to our year and then to see what the Master 11 adds to the mix.

The 11 is a double 1; all about the self, creativity, initiation, independence, innovation, and self-confidence. We just experienced a 1 Universal Year in 2017; an intense year of rebirth, new beginnings, and initiation. Yet the foundational energy for the 11 is the 2; all about love, relating to others, partnership, patience, and being supportive. So, can you see how, if we're all feeling the energy of the 11 this year, we might feel somewhat conflicted most of the time? The core energy of the year resides in the number 2. Without the Master 11, the 2 Universal Year is a slower and patience-building year. It's energy offers slowdowns, delays, and some frustrations along the way. It's a year to slow the pace and instead place a focus on others rather than so directly on ourselves. The number 2 Universal Year focuses on love, emotions, and relationships.

2018 is a time to regroup and focus on love and relationships. It's a great year for getting to know ourselves better and to tap into our authentic emotional lives. It's a time where we will have heightened emotions and also a heightened intuitive sense. The vibe of the number 2 is diplomatic, meditative, loving, and emotionally attuned. Its optimal expression is patience, fair-mindedness, diplomacy, service, loving and being lovable.

The overall mission for all of us during this 11/2 Universal Year is to clarify the limits of our responsibility and learn to work in cooperation with harmony, balance, and mutual respect. Yet the Master numbers present us with conflicting agendas. Understand that "Master" means "Teacher." And the Master numbers prod all of us to "master" our lives in ways that are perhaps more elevated. When you work with a Master number, it's as though you're enrolled in a school for the gifted. And just to complicate matters, the energy of 2018 encourages— on top of the mission outlined by the number 2—us to use our creativity, intuition, and healing abilities for the benefit of humanity as a whole. The double 1 is all about leadership and confidence and the 2 is all about harmony and love. So this year might offer up some strange and conflicting experiences across the board. If you're astrologically inclined, you might deepen your connection with the number 11 by its association with the Chiron figure. We could nickname 2018 "The Year Of The Wounded Healer." Its energy offers deep and profound healing at a core level. Yet this "healing" might not be apparent from the outside. It's often an internal healing; a shift in perspective resulting in a reconfiguration of our core sense of reality and our place within it.

How to Harness The Power of the 11/2 Universal Year

2018 can continue to be a year of action, yet underneath it there will be delays, stoppages, and weird detours. Both determination and patience are requirements; a delicate balance of action and allowing. It's almost like the urgency when applying for a new job or starting a business. We'll need a plan, proper financing, and the tenacity to go with the flow of creation, which is rarely (if ever) a linear path. Remember that even when things are super-busy we will still be met with unexpected stoppages, slow-downs, and delays if not downright re-routing. It's a time to think on our feet and trust in some sense of timing and overall agenda.

Make it a double. Get ready for intensity across the board. The double 1's offer double the pleasure and double the challenges related to the number 1. This year continues to push all of us to step into our power, to find our sense of individuation, and to exert healthy independence. Yet the foundational energy is softer, more fluid, and all about connecting and integrating with others. So, it's certainly set up as a delicate balance, to be sure. Yet just knowing that the year offers a "teeter-totter" effect can provide us with ways to create optimal results for ourselves. When we can really dive into our intuitive sense of when to push for results (the energy of the 1) and then back off and wait (the energy of the 2), magical things can transpire. They just won't transpire in a way that fits into your planner.

Getting to know you.

While the world will continue buzzing around us at breakneck speed, the underlying energy resides in connecting within relationships. This is a time where all of us will be searching and cultivating our "tribe"; the folks we truly want to have around. It takes time and intention to divest from certain people who drain us or bog us down. This is the time to create a new support system of people who inspire and support us in being the best version of ourselves. And this doesn't happen overnight. This is a year of restructuring on a macrocosmic and microcosmic level. During this time, we

78

will be met with opportunities to dig deeply into ourselves and come to terms with who we really are; and to define it, develop it, and own it. And then the energy of the double pioneering 1 pushes us to lead and take some risks.

Love. Love. Love. Love vs. Fear has become a pressing theme. An 11/2 Universal Year highlights and intensifies this theme. Now more than ever the notion of love is being expanded upon and redefined.   Inclusive or exclusive? Us or them? Care for humanity or "us first"? The 2 is heart energy and 2018 will challenge all of us to determine for ourselves what that means for the world at large and for each of us individually.

Challenges with the 11/2 Universal Year

Crisis, anyone? If you were hoping for easy street in 2018, well . . . sorry. With the 11/2, it's all about experiencing intensely challenging circumstances and coming out the other side stronger, more spiritually evolved, and ready to help others. Illumination comes by experiencing darkness and opting for the light. 2018 will have many of us on our knees. It won't be easy or in any way comfortable, yet it's profoundly deep and gratifying to move through crisis and remain standing. Collectively we're learning to understand that the "butterfly effect" we have on people is immeasurable.

Under pressure. Anytime we experience a Master number within a cycle we'll experience a heightened sense of anxiety. If we can understand this at the get-go, we can be kinder to ourselves and also extend a certain level of space to others throughout the year. If you're feeling edgy, chances are, so are other people. If you're feeling overwhelmed, chances are so are other people. If you're feeling enraged, chances are so are other people. It's a pressure-cooker this year and so we'll all benefit if we allow some wiggle room for ourselves and for others across the board. Remember that the number 2 is the teacher of patience and diplomacy. The cruel joke about the number 2 is that its power is also its biggest challenge. The number 2 teaches love, patience, and diplomacy and yet what must transpire for these important lessons to be learned? That's right, conflict. Therefore, when we're experiencing a cycle guided by the number 2, we'll find ourselves in more situations that require healthy emotional detachment and rational discernment. This is a year where we'll all be asked to back off and gain some distance from our own staunch viewpoints and attempt to see all sides of the equation in order to formulate win-win scenarios rather than win-lose outcomes.

Overall the 11 Universal Year brings a spotlight to the world in the realms love, diplomacy, leadership, and individuality. It's not necessarily an easy brew and yet its power is electrifying. The year brings opportunities for some visionary ideas and ideals to begin to take shape. It's earmarked for all of us to take a deep look at how we love and how we want to be loved. This is a perfect time for the cleansing of some deeply etched and outdated belief systems, to be examined for what they are and for there to be a "group" decision to retire the destructive norms and begin to replace them with upgraded paradigms that lift all of us in the world into a more harmonious state of being. This will transpire on every level; politically, environmentally, and in every other way, and in particular in our day-to-day relationships and activities.

Master Number 11 Numerology - The most intuitive

Numerology reduces all multi-digit numbers to the single-digit numbers 1 through 9 with the exception of the three Master numbers 11, 22 and 33. These three Master numbers in many cases are not reduced and have a specific set of attributes that sets them apart from all other numbers. Numerology enthusiasts and practitioners have always been especially excited about Master numbers because, as the name implies, they represent something above and beyond the mundane.

The 11 symbolizes the potential to push the limitations of the human experience into the stratosphere of the highest spiritual perception; the link between the mortal and the immortal; between man and spirit; between darkness and light; between ignorance and enlightenment. This is the ultimate symbolic power of the 11.

The secret lesson of the 11, a revelation you will not find in any Numerology book or article. Just as Numerology uses adding numbers, it also subtracts numbers looking for the difference between them; generally revealing what are called challenges or obstacles, and shortcomings you have to overcome.

Quite a few of us have an 11 among our core numbers. Does that mean that they have a better chance of reaching enlightenment? No, they do not. They have potential access to the attributes of the 11 such as intuition, but the story of the Master numbers as told above belongs in a different realm. There are those among us who do not have a single Master number in their chart and yet they can and have reached the ultimate spiritual heights symbolized by the 11. There are some with and without Master numbers who truly experience with every breath the reality of living up to the promises of the 22. And, if you are not just extremely lucky, but also incredibly perceptive, you may, in this lifetime, have an opportunity to meet that most precious of human beings; the Master Teacher, and recognize him or her for what he or she is.

The story of the Master numbers plays on different levels. On a more commonplace level, Master numbers found in an individual's chart indicate the potential access to the attributes attached to those Master numbers; the fine-tuned intuition of the 11; the master builder potential of the 22; the extraordinary teaching abilities of the 33. It is up to the individual to reach that potential and many, but by no means all, do. Unfortunately, there is a downside to having one or more Master numbers in your chart. The nervous energy of the 11, the frustrations and disappointments of the 22, and the shy and insecure nature of a 33.

COLOURS associated with number 11

Silver, glossy white, and black are the colours of 11, signifying truth, latent and active, hidden and revealed. Violet also belongs to 11 and signifies the illumination which the Spirit gains through sorrow. 11 develops Soul power through loving, selfless service.

11 as a DAY NUMBER

The 11 is a Karmic number and those under its influence will experience many 'challenges' in their lifetimes.

It is also a 'Master Number', indicating that you will excel in any job where you help others. 11 Day Number individuals are drawn to assist others in their understanding of themselves, and often set themselves up as the 'fall guy' for others as their energies can rise above the mundane to excel on higher levels of spirituality and inner-knowing. 11s will sometimes sacrifice their time and energy in the pursuit of uplifting and enlightening others on a day to day basis.

11 Day Number people often spend much of their time with their minds on the esoteric and spiritual.

Highly intuitive, 11 Day Number people often feel isolated or 'different' from others around them.

11 as a DESTINY number

11s tend to lead a life of extremes and in their quest to find a balance between the rational and the irrational, they will often pursue the most eclectic of religions and cultures.

These avant-garde and visionary individuals make great students, psychics, mystics, healers, teachers, writers, musicians and artists.

Many of them are 'wounded healers' who at some point in their life suffer a devastating experience that propels them on the search for their personal spirituality.

However, along with these situations usually comes a lot of toxic emotional baggage and a harsh inner-critic. It takes many 11's their entire life to rid themselves of the chip on their shoulder and achieve enlightenment.

The 11 is a Master Spiritual Number, giving you great intuition and psychic abilities. You are here to help the world, and when you enter a room, there is an 'energy' about you. You have a great sense of humour, but you must protect your vulnerable nervous system to avoid bouts of depression.

Your challenge is to protect your energy levels.

Your purpose is to help heal the world in any way you can.

Loren Schmal
© 2018 Loren Schmal

Founder of CyberPA

The art of saying NO!

It's in the set-up.

by
Steve Rogers

'No', by its nature is a negative word. It implies rejection, it assumes a stoppage of flow. It leads to arguments. It creates unease.

"Would you like a pizza?" No. Not serious.

"Did I get the job?" No. Not nice, but not life ending.

"Will you marry me?" No. Ouch.

But these are once off no's that divert our lives into different directions.

The no to pizza helped me lose weight.

The no to the job set me on course to go to China and open up a whole new world I didn't know existed.

The no to marriage was lucky because it turns out he or she was a useless dolt anyway!

It's the insidious yes's that kill our lives in small increments.

"Right, I'm set for Saturday. Park Run at 8, yoga at 09h30, brunch with friends at 11, home at 1 to do a few chores, fix the shelf that's been staring at me for weeks and then out to dinner. That might be a perfect day until your brunch friend calls and says "Hi, can we turn brunch into breakfast at 9, my parents are coming over about their holiday and they can't come earlier ..."

"No!" plays through your mind.

"Why!" plays through your mind as their response.

"I've got stuff on" plays through your mind. 9 will kill Park Run and yoga.

And, if you're a friendly extrovert as I am and you enjoy time with your friends, it's oh so easy to say … YES, ok …"

This is a tiny example and many would argue it's a no brainer. Say "no, it doesn't suit us, we had an agreement for 11 and we can't make 9".

True, but what are friends for? Doesn't friendship trump yoga or Park Run.

Yes and no.

It all comes down to **the set up**.

We've all had occasion to meet important or famous people. Did you notice how the arrival of the Mr Important was preceded by the organisation of everyone else. Mr Important is a vegan; we must ensure there's no dairy in the breakfast. She has to leave at 9. She drinks sparkling water. She needs to take a call at 08h30. And everyone runs.

In South Africa, we have politicians who arrive 2 hours late because they can. Give me a break! Who are these people and why does the voting public grovel at the feet of people who plainly don't have the slightest respect for them?

It's in the set up.

We have friends who cycle. We have friends who go hunting. We have friends who play golf.

When social arrangements are being made, the first questions out are: "when are you cycling, hunting, golfing. Our event, holiday, dinner will fit in with you. Why?

It's in the set up.

It comes down to how seriously the members of a social or work group take their membership to another group.

For example: If I'm studying an MBA and I'm working late nights and weekends, then my time is important and not to be trifled with. But if I'm studying Seth Godin's marketing course online, that's irrelevant. It's not recognised.

If I'm practising for a 90km marathon, that's important and my 15km run is not to be interrupted by friends and family. Dinner will be at 8, not 18h30 because Jonny will finish his run at 7. "Do you know; he's going for silver?" Sighs of admiration fill the room and mommy / daddy / wife / sister / puffs up with pride.

But if I'm running a 5km time trial, that's entirely optional. Even if I do a mean 18'52".

It's in the set up.

In order to comfortably say "No", the receiver of the No is expecting a valid reason: "I'm going to yoga" doesn't cut it. "I'm training to become a yoga master" cuts it. So, when my friend at the beginning asks about moving brunch to breakfast, the easy No is "So sorry, can't, I'm at yoga as part of my master training". "Oh, ok, no problem, we'll make a new plan". No accepted. Comfortably.

It's in the set up.

The art of saying no is simply based on the commitment we have to our activities. If you run 10 kms 3 times a week and run marathons on weekends, people don't mess with your time and accept no without frustration.

Which really sums up our lives. If we want to make an impact on the world, be successful (however you prefer to define that) and grow as individuals and families, we have to commit to our chosen activities in a more formal way.

Yoga once a week, missed every 3rd week doesn't cut it. Running 5kms once a week doesn't cut it.

Besides the level of activity, the other key is fixed commitment. If you're studying Seth Godin's "The Marketing Seminar" online (as I am), it's not good enough to pay attention now and then. You have to communicate to family and friends that you're not available Monday nights from 8-10, as you are studying with Seth Godin! Jokes aside, online learning is not for the faint hearted. It's all too easy to laugh it off tonight and do it tomorrow night because it isn't live.

Exactly for that reason, you need to commit a fixed day and a time to sit and study or do whatever it is you've committed to doing. Otherwise, you become part of the 60%[1] or more of people who don't complete their online courses.

To summarise: saying no is an art if you feel the need for it to be so. It's a no brainer if you fill your diary with commitments to yourself and your family in a way that others take seriously.

Then you become Mr or Ms Important! And you might even get the bottled sparkling water you so deserve!

[1] http://blog.teachable.com/increase-course-completion-rates

Steve Rogers

© 2018 Steve Rogers

Steve Rogers works with committed and hands on leaders and managers; and assists them to put the right people in the right jobs.

Why others should be happy when you say NO

One of the most common reasons why people want to learn how to say no and set some clear boundaries for themselves, is because they feel stressed out, overwhelmed or run down all the time. They realise that in order to feel better, they need to address their workload.

However, setting boundaries is scary, and we have all sorts of excuses readily available for ourselves to keep us from saying no. We may miss out on that big promotion at work if we don't put in the extra hours. We will lose that big client, if we don't do what they ask us to do immediately. We will disappoint our family when we don't show up on their party... Sounds familiar?

But have you ever really seriously considered the upside of saying no, as much as the excuses for not saying it? Let's have a look at that:

- We tend to think that we can accomplish more when we work more hours. And this is true to some extent, as of course you will be able to do more in two hours then in just one hour. But, there is a limit to this. Research shows that this limit may differ depending on various factors (age, the work that you do, how active your personal life is, etc.), but on average this limit lies somewhere between 40-50 hours of work per week. When we work more than this number of hours per week, we get tired, lose focus, forget or oversee important things and we make mistakes. Fatigue impacts our physical and cognitive functioning. And this doesn't only happen to us during those extra hours that we put in, but it also affects those first 40-50 hours that we were working.

In short, our productivity spirals downwards fast, when we put in too many hours. A former boss of me once said: "On some days, I'm most productive when I'm enjoying a cold drink out in the sun and do absolutely nothing". And he was right; recharging is as important to productivity as working is!

- We tend to trust that karma will help us when we put in the extra effort or go the extra mile. When we are nice to people, people will be nice to us. When we help out in times of need, they will be there for us when we need them. When we work extra hard, we will get that promotion or land that big deal. And yes, that could all very well be true. But it may also backfire on you. When you are the person who's always offering help and support, others won't regard you as being "needy", and may completely overlook your need for their help or support. When you put in too much work and start hitting that downward spiral mentioned before, what do you think your boss or client will notice? All the effort that you've put in, or those less desirable results that came out?

- We tend to think that we please others the most by saying yes to their requests. People will love us for being so helpful, caring and attentive, right? No, wrong! When we feel stressed, tired or overwhelmed, we may get cranky, overreact, be less engaged in our interactions with others, or even become less interested in others full stop. And that's apart from the fact that our help or support may not entirely meet the other person's standards. Have you ever tried setting painting a door or baking a cake in such a state? Chances are that you first had to clean up a huge mess, and then had to start all over again. I once drove to a wedding, feeling stressed and exhausted. I never reached it, because I couldn't find the location, and it took me an hour longer to get back home again because I missed an exit on the motorway. And I became an unreliable no-show when people had counted on me to be there, which of course is worse than politely rejecting an invite in the first place.

We live with lots of assumptions, and these assumptions may not always be accurate. Stepping back for a moment and taking a helicopter view may help us to test our assumptions, especially if those assumptions aren't serving us (anymore).

Learning new behaviours, such as setting boundaries and saying no, will become a lot easier when we see the value of it not only for ourselves but also for others.

Dear Amarantine team,

When I learned that you would focus on saying no in your next issue, I wondered if you could help me. I find it extremely difficult to say no, and especially to my loved ones. I was born and raised with the idea that it's important to help each other when people are in need, and I really value being there for the people whom I love.

But... I hardly have any time for myself, and now as I'm getting a bit older, I am tired all the time. I know I need to make some changes, but I don't want to let my loved ones down either. How could I take this forward without selling anyone short?

Sandra Vanderwilt, Cape Town, South Africa

Dear Sandra,

When you've always said yes, people will have come to rely on you for your help and support, and as such they may be surprised, disappointed or even get angry when you all of a sudden start saying no. And that makes it even harder to say no and stick to it, as you didn't want to let them down in the first place.

But what happens if you don't learn to say no, and continue down the path of always saying yes. You will likely become even more tired and you might even become sick as a result of completely draining all of your energy reserves. And by that point, you'll be forced to say no because you simply can't do a yes anymore. You can be sure that this would be a bigger let down to everyone else, and even more importantly, to yourself!

Therefore, you'll need to learn how to manage your energy better, so that you can also continue to say yes at times when that is really important to you. And that really isn't about learning how to say no to all others, but it's more about learning how to say yes to yourself and acknowledging that your own needs are equally as important as those of all others.

So, what can you do to bring back more balance between your needs and those of all others? My suggestion would be to take a multi-angle approach:

- Acknowledge that your own energy is important, and start mapping out some time in your diary for yourself. Preferably, plan some things that really excite and energise you, and which can't easily be rescheduled or cancelled.

  By actually scheduling your "me-time", you can simply say to others "sorry, I can't do that, as I have these plans", which sounds different from just no, and takes the edge of it for yourself as well.

- Make sure to tell your loved ones that you have been feeling tired lately as a result of taking on a bit too much, and let them know which great things you've planned to re-energise and when. Share your excitement about your plans.

Your loved ones will likely feel that you really deserve to have some fun too, especially considering all the support that you've always provided. Knowing that you've made these other plans which you are really excited about, will put up a natural boundary for them to ask for your help. It doesn't mean that they'll never ask again, but likely they'll become a bit more selective with the requests that they put in, and they will start planning it around your plans instead of you adjusting your diary to their needs.

- And finally, learn to say no in a way that works for you. A simple no is an answer in itself, and doesn't need further clarification or explanation, but some of us may never feel comfortable with just saying no. Experiment with all the different ways that we can set our boundaries, and see what works and feels right for you. Some examples you may want to try:
  o Say no, and immediately offer an alternative solution;
    - "I can't help you, but I will give this person a call to see if they can help".
    - "I can't help you with this today, but I can help you next week".
    - "I can't help you, but I've heard some great reviews of this company that offers some great value support with this".
  o Say no, and provide an explanation / justification;

- "With my health issues, I'm afraid that I really can't do this anymore".
- "I wish I could be of help, but my diary is fully booked for the next two weeks."
  - Say no to part of the request;
    - "I can't be there all week, but I can free up Thursday to help you out"
    - "I can't help you redecorate the entire house, but I'm happy to sow the new curtains for you"
  - Postpone your decision, to allow yourself some extra time to come up with your decision and an answer that you feel happy and confident about:
    - "I'll have to check my diary, and will let you know tomorrow"
    - "I'll discuss our plans with my partner, and get back to you afterwards"

I hope this guidance will be helpful for you, and I would love to hear how things are working out for you, once you have practiced with some or all of the above.

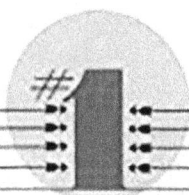

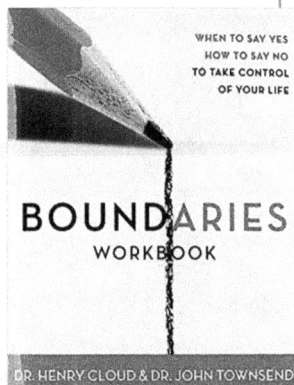

Welcome to your Personal & Professional Development with Amarantine

Amarantine supports your Personal and Professional Development through assessing, exploring, developing, and inspiring yourself to increase your self-awareness, self-knowledge, self-confidence, and self-esteem; to help you identify and develop your talents, skills, knowledge, competence, and experience to fulfil your personal aspirations in both your personal and professional life, to provide you with an enhanced lifestyle and improved quality of life as a result.

Whether you have a personal goal or a professional career goal, Amarantine will answer the questions you ask in an inspirational manner that helps you take the next step to achieve your own personal and professional aspirations.

Amarantine supports lifelong learning; which is achieved through both formal and informal learning processes. Formal learning is defined as education and training; whereas informal learning comes from coaching, mentoring, supervision, as well as things you experience, see, and hear in your everyday life.

Amarantine will inspire you to consciously learn and develop in all areas of your personal and professional life.

www.Amarantine.Life